CHRIST
All-Sufficient

CHRIST
All-Sufficient

The Unveiling of the Messiah in John 1–12

PAUL GRIEVE

CHRISTIAN MISSIONS IN MANY LANDS, Inc.
P. O. Box 13, Spring Lake, NJ 07762

Published by Christian Missions in Many Lands, Inc.
P. O. Box 13
Spring Lake, NJ 07762

ISBN 1-893579-03-4

Cover design by J. B. Nicholson, Jr.

Printed in the United States of America

Christ possessed by faith here
is young heaven and glory in the bud.

SAMUEL RUTHERFORD

Preface

It is a joy for me to introduce Paul Grieve's written ministry to Christians in North America and beyond. I had the good pleasure of meeting Paul and his wife, Dorothy, in September, 1997, and of enjoying the kind hospit ality of their home. In that brief period, a warm bond of friendship was forged.

Paul and Dorothy very kindly accepted an invitation to attend our Annual Conference for Missionaries while they were visiting Canada in 1998. Paul's ministry at the conference was based on the examples and results of disbelief in the first twelve chapters of John's Gospel. Certainly all of us are afflicted from time to time with doubts, fears and, dare we admit, moments of unbelief. Paul's ministry was so timely, practical, and at the same time, reaffirming. It was felt it should be shared with as many Christians as possible.

We are grateful to Paul for his ready agreement to have these messages printed.

Paul and Dorothy Grieves were commended by assemblies in Holywood and Donegall Road in Northern Ireland in 1968. They served the Lord in Zambia for almost fifteen years; first at Loloma where they studied the Luvale language, then later at Kabompo.

In 1983 they moved to Murchison Hospital in South Africa where Paul served as a medical technologist; however, as opportunities for ministry expanded to include numerous Bible studies, religious classes in the local high school, and ministry in other assemblies further afield, he was led to give up hospital duties and devote his full attention to the Lord's work.

Dorothy is responsible for a very busy and fruitful Emmaus work for Zulu-speaking students.

They have two children, both married, and living in South Africa.

SAMUEL ROBINSON
CMML
Wall, New Jersey
July, 1999

Foreword

Each year CMML (Christian Missions in Many Lands), a missionary service group based in New Jersey, holds a conference in Pennsylvania for missionaries who happen to be home on furlough. A relaxing time of fellowship is provided in the delightful surroundings of the Greenwood Hills Conference Center. Coupled with this, devotional ministry from the Word of God gives an opportunity for some respite for those who have been under the stress of constantly giving out from the Scriptures over an extended period of time.

It was my immense privilege to be invited to share some ministry from the Scriptures at the Missions Conference in 1998. Subsequently, Mr. Sam Robinson, the President of C.M.M.L., suggested that the talks should be put into written form and arranged for transcripts to be made from the tapes. This booklet is the revision of these talks in a form that, it is hoped, will be a blessing to any who may take time to read it.

I would like to express my sincere thanks to those who gave of their time and expertise. My good friend and colleague, Dr. Terry Gilpin and his wife, Jane, both expended much time and a good deal of red ink in making corrections to the manuscript and made many helpful suggestions. Most of these have been incorporated into the finished product. I am also most grateful to my dear wife who gave me much help and encouragement.

Finally, and above all else, I must record my gratitude to our glorious Lord Who has so faithfully cared for us over the past 31 years since we first ventured out in service to Him. If His Name is not glorified in the production of this booklet, then the time and effort expended will have been in vain. On the other hand, if what is written serves to draw some dear saint's heart closer to the Savior, then I will have been amply repaid for the effort made.

PAUL R. GRIEVE
Murchison
February 1999

Table of Contents

Introduction

In Matthew 13 the Lord Jesus spoke of a scribe whom He portrayed as a householder who brings forth out of his treasure things new and old. I suppose in our various ministries each of us delves into the Word of God for thoughts, for gems, for messages, for instruction, for guidance, for something to feed and challenge our own souls and then to pass on to others. More often than not, what we pass on are *things old*, with just a scattering of *things new*. Then we may discover, to our horror, that the new things really were old things we had heard, perhaps years previously, and had forgotten. There is nothing new under the sun. I imagine that everything I am going to say will be very much old hat, but although it is old, I trust it will not be stale. The old things can be very precious.

Let's have a little look at the Gospel of John. We are all aware that this gospel is divided into three main sections. The first 12 chapters are quite distinct from the rest of the book. In them, the Lord Jesus is dealing with people—different individuals, different groups, and just people in general. At chapter 13, we find an abrupt change. The section from chapter 13 to the end of chapter 16 is often referred to as "The Upper Room Ministry" of the Lord. Taking chapters 13 through 16 as a unit, we see that the Lord is being very personal, talking to His disciples and, in chapter 17 of course, speaking to His Father. In chapters 18 to 21, it is a distinctly different type of narrative: the arrest and trial; the crucifixion; the ascension. Therefore, we can see that these three sections of the gospel are very distinct.

We are going to consider incidents in the first 12 chapters of this gospel where the Lord is presenting Himself as a Prophet[1].

As we go through these chapters and pick out some of the pertinent events, I hope our hearts will thrill again and again as we see how the Lord puts His finger on the problems of life and how the answer to these is provided in our wonderful Savior.

We are all aware that John has certain favorite words he uses very frequently. One of the most prominent of these is the word "believe." It occurs repeatedly—in fact, John uses the word 100 times in his gospel. (He also uses the word in his epistles but never in the book of Revelation.) Remarkably, on average in his gospel, John uses the word believe once in every nine verses. Clearly, belief is a subject in which John is very interested.

I would like to look at these chapters from a different perspective. We will examine together *unbelief* in these first 12 chapters of John's gospel. This word does not occur in this section of the Scriptures. John never uses it—not even once! Why, then, does he use the word believe so much? I think it is because unbelief was so rife that he had to use the word believe an enormous number of times to get his message across and to counter the unbelief that was so prevalent.

Unbelief, then, is the topic we are going to consider. That may sound to be a most unsuitable subject, but I trust that what we have to say will be a help and a blessing.

Hebrews 3:12 says:

> *Take heed, brethren, lest there be in any of you an evil heart of unbelief, in departing from the living God.*

I am taking that verse right out of context—I know that. The verse has to do with those Jewish believers in that early period of the church when they were under extreme pressure to go back into Judaism. That is the context of the verse. Nevertheless, I do believe that perhaps we need that little injunction from time to time. Speaking personally, I know that in our thirty years of trying to serve the Lord in little ways here and there, from time to time we have found ourselves in what might be described as distressing circumstances, with overwhelming problems. In such situations, it is easy to allow unbelief to creep in and feel that perhaps it is just not worth while carrying on. We will see, as we look through these first 12 chapters of John's gospel, that whatever the circumstances of life, the Lord Jesus Christ is the complete and perfect answer to what we are facing.

ENDNOTE

1 It is interesting to note that in the first 12 chapters, the word *prophet* is used 14 times, and yet from chapter 13 to the end of the book it is not used once. Thus, we deduce that in those twelve chapters the Lord Jesus is being presented as a Prophet, the One who has come from God to the people with a message. In chapters 18–21, the last section of the book, the word *king* occurs 12 times, while it only occurs four times in the first twelve chapters. So this emphasis in the last section would suggest to us that here the Lord Jesus is presented to us as a King, rejected, but nonetheless glorious because He rises from the dead. In the center section, where the Lord is speaking to His disciples and (in ch. 17) to His Father, He is, of course, a Priest. This is particularly seen in chapter 17 where He is interceding for His disciples in the presence of His Father. So in these three sections of the Gospel of John we have the Lord Jesus presented as a Prophet, a Priest, and a King.

The Darkness of Unbelief

Speaking of the Lord Jesus Christ, in John 1:4-5 John says:

In Him was life; and the life was the light of men. And the light shineth in darkness; and the darkness comprehended it not.

Where did this darkness come from? The darkness is a result of unbelief. Later, in verse 11, we read how the Lord Jesus came into this world: *"He came unto His own, and His own received Him not."* He came to His own things; literally, that is the meaning. Why does it say that? Because He made everything; He owns everything; they are His by right. He came into this world, not just to the people, but into the world, the whole situation of His creation. And His own people did not receive Him. The Jewish nation had the Word of God, the priests of God, the temple of God, the sacrifices of God—they had it all—and they did not receive Him. They were in darkness—the darkness of unbelief.

That is where the world is today. We know, of course, that the gospel of John was written to the world—it was written for everybody. But we also know that God chose that one nation of Israel as a representative of the whole world. Therefore, what is true of the nation is, in fact, true of the world. Moreover, what is true of the people in darkness in the world can tragically become true of us if we are not very careful.

Let me ask a question. Look back over your life now, since you trusted the Lord and since you have been in His service. Have there ever been times when you have been groping to find the way ahead? You are not sure what the Lord has in store for you. There appears to be a cloud, a darkness that obscures the path. Why is it so? Perhaps it is because it is incredibly difficult to walk constantly and unerringly in the light. Why is this so? It is because in our hearts there is a tendency to drift toward the darkness. Our old sinful nature feels more comfortable in those things. Consequently, when we find ourselves groping, stumbling, and not making our way forward, it may be because we are not as close to the Lord as we should be.

I am sure you have found, as we have over the years, that people tend to set missionaries up on a pedestal and think they are always "super-spiritual." That is horrendous because we all know that we are very far from that. We all experience times when we wake up one day to discover that we have got out of touch with the Lord and find ourselves groping in the darkness.

Of course, the wonderful thing is we are not like the people in the world because we have access to the light of God's presence. Look at verse four: *"In Him was life; and the life was the light of men."* To what life is John referring? He is referring to Christ's life. What is His life? It is eternal life, a life that never had a beginning and will never have an end. It is the life of God that has been given to you and me. And that life is the light of men. We do not need to walk in darkness! Isn't that glorious? There is a Savior who comes into our lives and, in the darkness, when we are groping and stumbling around, He sheds light on the path. He gives us direction. That is fantastic! I am sure you have experienced it as we have. When suddenly I wake up to the fact that I have drifted a little bit from the Lord into the dark shadows and just come back into the light again, I come before Him and start all over again. What a relief, what a glorious thing it is, to see the light on the pathway! From time to time, we need to take stock so that we are in the light, and enjoying that light.

Years ago, back home in Ireland, one of our overseeing brethren had a number of interesting phrases he used repeatedly. One of these was: "How wonderful it is to bask in the sunshine of His presence." That is good. It is lovely when we can relax and really soak up the warmth and beauty of God's sunlight. We can do the same in a spiritual sense. So here we have the darkness of unbelief, but we do not have to endure this because we have the Savior, who is the light, living within us.

The Barrenness of Unbelief

In John 1:23, we have another spotlight. This time it is focused on John the Baptist who said:

> *I am the voice of one crying in the wilderness, Make straight the way of the Lord, as said the prophet Isaiah.*

John the Baptist was a wonderful character. If asked to choose a phrase to write over his life, virtually every one of us would, I suppose, select: *"He must increase, I must decrease"* (Jn. 3:30). That really sums up this great man of God—and he was a great man of God; the Lord Jesus said so. However, I want to put a different phrase over John the Baptist for the purposes of what we are going to consider. I am going to write over him: *"the voice of one crying in the wilderness."* John, of course, literally came in the wilderness, preaching to the people of Israel, and that is what he meant. He was a voice crying in the wilderness, the desert of Judea.

What is a wilderness? South Africa is a land with many different types of ground. We live among the rolling hills of southern Natal, brilliant green with a luscious growth of sugar cane and tea plantations. You can travel mile after mile and find endless rolling hills of green fertile soil. If you keep traveling south, eventually, about a thousand miles later, you come to Cape Town. But before you get there, you may travel through the Karoo Desert. Deserts are strange places with seemingly endless miles of wasteland—empty, barren, rocky, stony, sandy with a few bits of scrub here and there. It is still earth, still this world in which we are living, and still the same country. Oh, but so different from Natal! The fertile ground has given way to barren land.

The distinction between fertile land and barren land is not at all subtle. Barren land is not merely not producing fruit; it is incapable of it. Fertile land may, or may not, produce fruit, but it has the capacity to do so.

John was in the wilderness, a barren desert incapable of producing fruit. Ah, but John was talking about something more important than the agricultural phenomenon of the desert! Isaiah 53:1-2 says,

> *Who hath believed our report? and to whom is the arm of the Lord revealed? For He shall grow up before Him as a tender plant, and as a root out of a dry ground.*

To whom is Isaiah referring? He is referring to the Lord Jesus. He was a root out of a dry ground. What was the dry ground? It was the dry ground of Judaism. Those people had become spiritually barren. In their spirits, they were as barren as the wilderness in which John was preaching. The lives that once held the promise of producing much fruit for God had become unfruitful and ultimately degenerated into barrenness.

Have you ever had a barren period in your life? I certainly have—too often! But the Bible says that the desert shall blossom as a rose. And if God can make the barren soil of the desert produce beautiful fragrant flowers, He can do the same in the barren soul of His child. We have proved that repeatedly, haven't we? This is the barrenness of unbelief. Our Savior can come in and turn that whole situation around so that we become fruitful for God. How marvelous! It is really wonderful that God can take the likes of me, a nobody, who knows nothing, and sometimes produce just a little bit of fruit here and there. That is astounding, but it is what He wants to do, and it is what He does when we let Him.

John says, "I am a *voice.*" There is something very peculiar about a voice. You cannot see it. You can only hear it. In fact, when John says "*I am the voice...crying in the wilderness,*" he is really saying the same as when he said, *"He must increase and I must decrease."* He says, "I am a *voice.* You do not see me. Christ has increased so much that you do not see me. I am crying in the wilderness." What is he crying? *"Prepare ye the way of the Lord."* He is talking about the Lord, directing their attention to Him. Here we have the whole crux of the matter.

What brings barrenness to our souls? Isn't it when we get our eyes off the Lord? We get our eyes onto the wilderness around us. Perhaps we get involved with pressures and problems that we would rather leave alone, but because of the nature of the work we have no choice but to be involved with them. We would rather be doing something else, like the missionary who said, "I used to sit in my study trying to get into the Word and there would be a knock on the door. After dealing with the interruption and getting back to the study, there would be another knock and I would be interrupted again. I used to get so frustrated with all these interruptions to my work, until one day I discovered that the interruptions *were* my work!" Yes, we can get frustrated and the frustration can bring barrenness. The problem is that too often we are looking at ourselves. It is *my* work; *I* am being interrupted; why can they not let *me* get on with it? It is all I, I, I. I am no longer a voice: I am the important one. John says, "I'm a voice, only a voice; not worth very much, but I want to direct you to Someone who is worthy to be the center of attention—to the Savior," and the barrenness will disappear. He makes the desert blossom as a rose. How lovely this is!

The Joylessness of Unbelief

Moving to John 2:1-3, we read:

And the third day there was a marriage in Cana of Galilee, and the mother of Jesus was there: and both Jesus was called, and His disciples, to the marriage. And when they wanted wine, the mother of Jesus saith unto Him, they have no wine.

This incident in the life of the Lord Jesus, where He performed His very first miracle, is another picture of the nation of Israel. Here it represents the joylessness of unbelief. Wine in the Scriptures is a picture of joy. It is *"wine that maketh glad the heart of man"* (Ps. 104:15). Unbelief brings joylessness. We can see it in the world all around us. Unbelief brings nothing but sorrow, despair, and bitterness.

Here is a marriage. It should be the happiest day in the life of this couple, but the source of joy has dried up. What is a marriage anyway? It is something that God invented and ordained for people. It is not an ordinance of the church. It is something that God has designed, because God knows that it is only within the bonds of matrimony we can live on earth with real joy in such intimate relationships. So when a man and a woman are brought together in marriage, this should be such a joyous occasion. It is a picture of that very special, inexplicable relationship we should have with the Lord, and there is no joy like that. If it is impossible to describe in words just what marriage means, how much more impossible is it to describe the union of a soul with the Savior and the joy that should flow from that. But the wine failed.

This event is right at the beginning of their married life.

They are just starting out; they have hardly begun. They are stuck there in that marriage celebration, and before they get away from the crowd to be on their own, the wine dries up. So often Satan strikes right at the very beginning of our experience with Christ. And not only that but so often when we have a very special time with the Lord and really feel close to Him, suddenly we lose that sense of His presence. Satan attacks in some way. Of course, for each individual he will attack in a different way. There is also the possibility that it might not even be Satan. We blame an awful lot on Satan, and it is not always his fault. Whatever the origin of the problem, the wine has dried up—the joy is lost.

Mary said to Jesus, *"They have no wine."* Why did she say that to Him? Of course, she did not need to tell the Lord! He knew perfectly well there was no wine. He knew it better than she did, but she said it nonetheless. Was Mary also trying to find her feet? She had lived with the Lord for thirty years, acting as His mother. He was just entering His public ministry. Have you ever wondered what Mary thought as the Lord Jesus was growing up? Here was the perfect child. Now I know that your children are the perfect children—at least, at times we fondly imagine that our children are just *perfect.* But Mary did not have to imagine anything. Her child was perfect! He was the one child who never broke a toy, never threw a tantrum, never spoke a word back to His mother. Isn't that true? He was the one child in the whole world who never picked a fight with others in the family. The one child who never had to say, "I'm sorry." Mary watched all this. She saw it and she knew very well the significance of it all, but maybe she was still learning to cope with that. She went to the Lord and said, *"They have no wine."* She was expecting something, wasn't she?

The Lord had never done a miracle before, but Mary knew by experience that if there was an answer He would have it. She did not know what He was going to do but she said, *"They have no wine."* Isn't that a lesson for us? "Lord, I've no joy, I've lost the wine of joy in my life." Oh, she went to the right person, and He resolved the whole situation! When we find that we have lost our joy, we know to whom we should go to have the problem resolved.

Look again at verse 11:

> *This beginning of miracles did Jesus in Cana of Galilee, and manifested forth His glory; and His disciples believed on Him.*

Not only did the Lord Jesus speak words that were different, but also He did things that were different. His actions were completely contrary to ours.

Let us think for a moment of a young man making his debut as a concert pianist. He plays his Mozart and his Rachmaninov, his Beethoven and his Chopin. At the end he comes to a grand finale and the beautiful, flowing music comes to a great, crashing crescendo. The people are on their feet, shouting, cheering, whistling, stamping, clapping, and calling for an encore. They are giving him glory—something he never had before. This is his first time to receive such accolades and he is going to have to work very hard to keep that standard up in order to get more and more glory.

However, it says here, Jesus *"manifested forth His glory,"* They were not *giving* Him glory: He was showing them the glory that was always there within Him! When people do wonderful things, they are attracting a glory that they do not have within themselves. The next morning, of course, in the newspapers there is the review of the concert and more glory is added to the young man. But our Lord is not like that. The glory is His. It is inherent in Him, and He is just revealing a tiny little bit of it. He does not have to work up something to gain it, and then keep working hard to get some more glory the next time. He is just revealing a little bit more of what is already there. That is what the Gospel of John is all about. John unfolds and reveals more, and more of the glories of Christ, of His compassion, of His deity, of His knowledge, of His wisdom: His glories are gradually being unfolded, a little bit at a time.

But, oh, the people with whom He had to work! This is the contrast we see between the Lord and the people. Those people are like you and me. We have looked at the *darkness of unbelief* and how that darkness can only be dispelled by the glorious person of the Lord Jesus Christ. We have seen the *barrenness of unbelief* and we found that it is only Christ who can make the desert of our spiritual experience blossom as a rose. We have seen, in the marriage of Cana of Galilee, the *joylessness of unbelief* and it was only the Lord Jesus who was capable of restoring what should have been there. It is amazing the number of different things that can come into our lives that do not need to be there. We can allow them to get there, but while the world does not have a choice, we do have a choice; we have the Savior. We do not need to carry on in the darkness, in barrenness, or in joylessness when these things do invade our lives.

The Hypocrisy of Unbelief

The next event we will consider is found in John 2:13-16.

> *And the Jews' passover was at hand, and Jesus went up to Jerusalem, and found in the temple those that sold oxen and sheep and doves, and the changers of money sitting: and when He had made a scourge of small cords, He drove them all out of the temple, and the sheep, and the oxen; and poured out the changers' money, and overthrew the tables; and said unto them that sold doves, "Take these things hence; make not My Father's house an house of merchandise."*

What an interesting event this is at the very beginning of the Lord's ministry. Let us not forget that these are God's chosen people and they are doing what God told them to do: they are having a Passover feast. These people are in the temple, the very place in which God had directed they should gather to worship Him and to offer sacrifices. These are religious people; they are good people. These are God's people. They are doing the right thing, in the right place, at the right time—that is, as far as observing the Passover is concerned.

The problem is that it was all for effect: "Do you see how good we are? We are keeping the Passover; we are in the temple; we are God's people; we have the law: we, we, we…" But they have added, added, added. What have they added? Let us think it through for a moment. There was a Passover feast, so they needed Passover lambs. They no longer had an agricultural community. Instead, the people were living in the cities. They did not have sheep so lambs had to be provided for them. Then there were the Jews coming from various countries of the Roman world (they are listed for us in Acts 2). They were coming with Roman currency for, in the Roman Empire, shekels were not legal tender. Shekels must be provided for them with which to buy the animals. "Do you not realize that we are providing a service for the people of God?" they might have said. Does this sound familiar? Let me explain what is on my mind.

We who are missionaries are in danger of thinking along these lines: "Don't you people realize that we've come here to help you? Don't you know what we've given up for you?" Did you ever think like that? No, we are no longer like John the Baptist, are we? We are no longer a voice telling others to look at the Lord! Rather, we are saying, "Look at us; look at what we've left; look at what we're doing." Can we not see the incongruity of it all?

These people were in the temple, providing a service for those coming to worship, encouraging them to do the right thing. Actually, it was all just a front. This is the *hypocrisy of unbelief*. They were not really so much interested in providing shekels for the foreigners as in the exchange rate. Moreover, they were not really interested in providing sheep for a Passover sacrifice; they had their eye on the profit margin. That is hypocrisy. Sometimes we can wake up one day to realize we have been going through the motions for weeks, and we have not even met with the Lord. We have done our Bible study. We have had our times of prayer. We have done our preaching, or whatever it is we have to do, and maybe it is all a big front.

If there is one thing God hates, it is hypocrisy. How do I know? Didn't we read about it here? The Lord Jesus made a whip and turned those people out without ceremony or apology! This almost seems to be out of character, but it is not. It is merely another side to this wonderful Person whom we love.

Did you notice how everything He did was toned down just a little bit? It is not that He was condoning what they were doing. I remember seeing in one of the modern translations a line drawing depicting this scene. The animals were being whipped out, the tables were falling over, the money was being scattered everywhere, and the doves were flying away. But the Lord did not do that, did He? Referring to the doves, He said, *"Take these things hence."* They could go and round up the sheep and the oxen afterwards and reclaim them, but if He let the doves go, they would have been permanently lost. It is truly wonderful how the Lord thought of every tiny detail even when He was dealing with these rascals. Indeed, I would not be surprised if it were these very people who were at the forefront, a few years later, shouting out, *"Crucify Him, crucify Him."* The hypocrisy of unbelief is a terrible thing. There is not a single one of us that would condone hypocrisy for half a moment. We despise it and, in our heart of hearts, would flee from it. How we need the Word of God to search out our hearts so that we can deal with such insidious sins.

From time to time these things have been my experience and, I assume that because I am an average sort of person, you may also have had similar experiences. The beauty and glory of it all is that through the darkness, through the barrenness, through the joylessness, through the hypocrisy, there is the Savior just waiting to bring us out of that situation where we should not be so that we can enjoy His presence again.

The Dullness of Unbelief

Now let us go to John 3:10 to see further how unbelief has such a devastating effect on every single part of our being and our lives. We do not need to read the whole passage for we know it by heart! Verse 10 will be sufficient.

> *Jesus answered and said unto* [Nicodemus], *"Art thou a master of Israel and knowest not these things?"*

Here we have the *dullness of unbelief.* There is one thing, I think, that we need constantly to remind ourselves of, and it is this: mere intellect can never, ever come to a knowledge of God or His Word. I think we have all experienced that. Back home in South Africa there is a young man in our assembly, a converted Jew. Speaking of his life before he trusted the Lord, he often says, "How could I have been so blind?" He reads his Old Testament in Hebrew and says, "Why did I never see it like this before?" It is because intellectual study of the Word of God cannot reveal the truths of God. It takes the Spirit of God to reveal the truth of God. One of the great proofs that a person has truly trusted the Savior is when he has an appetite and an appreciation for the Word of God.

Here we are introduced to a man, Nicodemus, a teacher. Yet, he was not "*a* teacher!" If you look at the Greek text, it says "*THE* teacher in Israel." There is an interesting little point in John 8:44. The Lord Jesus says,

> *Ye are of your father the devil, and the lusts of your father ye will do. He was a murderer from the beginning, and abode not in the truth, because there is no truth in him. When he speaketh a lie, he speaketh of his own…*

That should read, "when he speaketh *the* lie." It is not just some little lie; it is *the* lie. Do you remember the Pharisee and the tax collector who went up to the temple to pray? The Pharisee was the one who was telling the Lord how good he was, how much he had done, and how he should be accepted. Then this poor tax collector, the publican, who would not even lift up his eyes to heaven, said, "God be merciful to me a sinner." Now, he did not say that! He said, *"God be merciful to me **the** sinner."* There is a sense in which *the lie* characterizes Satan and *the sinner* characterizes every truly repentant individual who comes to the feet of the Savior. We find that the Lord Jesus puts His finger on the character of Nicodemus. He was not just a teacher; he was *the* teacher. Evidently, he was the greatest teacher that Judaism could produce at that time. Nevertheless, he was dull; he did not understand. A mere intellectual approach to the Word of God by the worldling can never bring that person to a knowledge of Christ. It takes the working of the Spirit of God to open his heart, to open his mind, to open his eyes to reveal the Savior to him. It is because an intellectual study of the Scriptures is insufficient that we have multitudes of church leaders in Christendom who know nothing of Christ. I am not saying we should throw intellect out the window! God has given us intelligence and we must use it. What I am saying is that we need the Spirit of God to reveal the Word of God to us, otherwise we will be dull and will not understand.

In 1 Corinthians 2:12, we read,

> *We have received, not the spirit of the world, but the Spirit which is from God; that we might know the things that are freely given to us of God.*

Why did God give us His Spirit? One reason was if we did not have the Spirit of God, we could not know the things of God. We read in 1 Corinthians 2:13,

> *Which things also we speak, not in the words which man's wisdom teacheth, but which the Holy Spirit teacheth; comparing spiritual things with spiritual.*

Here again we see this same truth explicitly stated. Man's wisdom can neither apprehend nor pass on the truth of God. 1 Corinthians 3:14 states:

> *But the natural man* [that is, the unsaved man] *receiveth not the things of the Spirit of God: for they are foolishness unto him: neither can he know them, because they are spiritually discerned.*

And he is spiritually dead. This truth is emphasized repeatedly in this passage of Scripture.

But there is a problem here. It is quite clear that an unsaved person cannot understand the Scriptures unaided, but once a person has trusted the Lord, surely that is the end of the matter. Sadly, it is not! Let us look at 1 Corinthians 3:1-2.

> *And I, brethren, could not speak unto you as unto spiritual, but as unto carnal, even as unto babes in Christ. I have fed you with milk, and not with meat: for hitherto ye were not able to bear it, neither yet now are ye able.*

Here were true believers who had been wondrously saved, but had not made the progress necessary to understand the deeper things of the Spirit. We have the same in Hebrews 5:11-12. Speaking of Melchizedek, the writer says,

> *Of whom we have many things to say, and* [difficult to be explained], *seeing ye are dull of hearing. For when for the time ye ought to be teachers, ye have need that one teach you again which be the first principles of the oracles of God; and are become such as have need of milk, and not strong meat.*

Note the word *become,* showing that it is possible for us to have an understanding of the Word of God, given by the Spirit of God, and to *become* dull. This is the *dullness of unbelief.* Oh, it is very possible; we have all experienced it in our lives. It is only a vision of the Lord Jesus given to us by the Spirit of God that can remove that dullness, bring a clarity of thought and show us something of the truth of God.

The Dryness of Unbelief

The next little cameo is found in John 4:15 just one verse from that delightful story of the woman at the well. *"The woman saith unto Him, 'Sir, give me this water, that I thirst not, neither come hither to draw.'"* She said, *"Give me this water."* Here is a thirsty woman. This is the *dryness of unbelief.* Have you ever been dry? Spiritually dry? I think we all know what it is like. The problem is that when we are spiritually dry we can go to the wrong place to quench our thirst like the woman coming to the well. Of course, she was also physically dry—that is fair enough. However, the Lord is using this interview with the woman to reveal her deeper need, and then to reveal where her need could be met. Then the woman says, when she learns of her greater need, "Well, sir, you give me that water. That's really what I want." Did you notice, further down, in verse 28 it says, *"The woman left her water pot"*? Why did she leave it? She left it because she no longer had any need for it. Now she had something better.

It is interesting to see how the Lord Jesus deals differently with different people. Here is a woman whose life was an absolute mess. If there was anything she needed, it was new life. However, the Lord Jesus did not talk to her about new life. Isn't that remarkable? In the previous chapter, Nicodemus was an exemplar, the one of moral excellence in the community. The Lord Jesus talked to him about new life and the new birth. I would have thought the Lord would have talked to Nicodemus about worship; after all, he was a religious man, a leader, and the teacher in the Jewish community. It seems to be somehow out of place for the Lord to speak to this immoral woman about worship instead of the new birth.

Sometimes we try to adjust our message to the people, don't we? For example, we think like this: "The audience I will be speaking to will be comprised of university people so I must be a little bit intellectual to get their ear." The Lord was not like that. I would have thought that a discussion on worship with Nicodemus would have been a good starting point because it was, in a sense, common ground. On the other hand, I would not have thought worship was a subject to be discussed with an immoral woman! So you see, the Lord's ways are not our ways, and His thoughts are not our thoughts. Above and beyond anything else, we really need to be guided by the Spirit of God in dealing with people, and not merely use our intelligence. Of course, we must not abandon intelligence! What I mean is that we must not mistakenly allow our intelligence to take the place of the leading of the Spirit of God.

How easy it is to be dry, to get to the place where we have just nothing to give. Again, I think most of us have been there. How often is it when we are preparing before the Lord for a meeting or some other commitment that we feel dry? We find ourselves searching, searching, searching, but we get nothing fresh, nothing new. What do we need at such a time? We need what the Lord Jesus gave to this woman: a fresh vision of Himself.

If you were to put over this woman's head a little phrase to describe her and her experience, what would it be? I think I would choose verse 29 that says, *"Come see a man."* Here was a woman who had spent her life looking at men. Now she says, *"Come see a man."* Do you remember what Nicodemus said in John 3:2?

> *We know that Thou art a teacher come from God: for no man can do these miracles that thou doest except God be with him.*

Now the woman says: *"Come see a man."* I think later in his life Nicodemus did the same as the woman, but she got there first, despite the fact that she came from such a bad background. She then described the Lord as *"A man which told me...* " That is what we need. To get that freshness, that refreshment and quenching of our spiritual thirst, we need to come and see the Man who will tell us what we need to know. He will reveal Himself to us, as He revealed Himself to Nicodemus, to His disciples, to this woman, and to those people in the temple who were selling their goods. That is what God is doing with us, and in us. We cannot take too much at once, but He is constantly revealing Himself, a little at a time.

Why has He taken us onto the mission field? Oh, we would like to think it is so we can serve Him and bring others to a knowledge of Christ, and of course that is true. Ah, but there is something far more than that. All the circumstances of our lives are designed so that we can learn more of Christ. It is a learning process.

When we went to Zambia in 1968, we knew less than nothing. We were still very "wet behind the ears." We were really only children and the Lord started teaching us different things. After almost 15 years there I suppose we thought we knew one or two things. Then, when the Lord took us to South Africa, we discovered to our amazement that our 15 years in Zambia were just a training ground for what He had for us in South Africa! That has been an incredible lesson to learn. Now I am beginning to suspect that our 15 years in South Africa have been a training ground for something else that He has for us. I do not know. The truth is that our whole lives are a training ground for the future—whether the future here on earth, or our future service in glory. Isn't it true that our service in heaven will somehow be related to our faithfulness in service on earth? So our service is not an end in itself; it is a means toward an end. And what is that end? It is that Christ will be revealed to us, and through us to others. The *dryness of unbelief* can be a hindrance to this.

The Disease of Unbelief

Our next Scripture is John 4:46:

Jesus came again into Cana *of Galilee, where He made the water wine. And there was a certain nobleman, whose son was sick at Capernaum.*

This man's son was sick: the *sickness of unbelief*—another little facet of unbelief in the gospel of John. Sickness, of course, is disease. The word disease is very interesting. It is dis-ease. In other words, our bodies, which should be at ease and comfortable, are no longer at ease; something has gone wrong. This is disease.

Of course, we understand very clearly the question of sin in the unsaved person. In the sight of God, this is disease. In addition, in the Scriptures we have that horrible picture of leprosy, a graphic portrayal of what God sees when He looks at the soul of an unsaved person. But now that we are saved there is, in a spiritual sense, no longer disease. Is that true? Well, I do not think it is, because we can become very uncomfortable in our spirits when we drift a little bit from the Lord; and discomfort is disease.

Picture ourselves in the presence of God, reading the Scriptures. As we read, the Word of God enters our soul; and the entrance of His Word gives light (Ps. 119:130). The light shines right into the deep recesses of our hearts and reveals certain things that are there. Really, we would be much more comfortable if some of these things were not revealed! We are uncomfortable—at dis-ease. Sin has been exposed.

As we pursue this thought, there is a very interesting little verse I would like to share with you. It is 1 John 1:7:

> *If we walk in the light, as He is in the light, we have fellowship one with another, and the blood of Jesus Christ, His Son, cleanseth us from all sin.*

Now, I have a problem with this delightful verse. *"If we walk in the light, as He is in the light, we have fellowship one with another."* That is good; we understand that, and we enjoy it. We are having fellowship with each other, and fellowship is sweet. Why then does John bring in this question of sin? *"And the blood of Jesus Christ cleanses us from all sin."* Why does he say that? Surely, there can be no question of sin when we are having fellowship with one another, for sin breaks such fellowship. The answer is very simple. When we walk in the light, the light shows up what we would not otherwise see. So, as we walk in the light of the presence of the Lord and in the light of His Word, the Spirit of God, using the Word of God, reveals things in our hearts that just ought not to be there and we become uncomfortable. We must deal with those things. When we fail to deal with them, of course, is when the problem comes. However, if we do deal with them, then we are brought a little bit closer to the Lord. And because we are a little bit closer to the Lord, then the light shines that little bit more brightly, and shows up something else that needs to be dealt with! Have you ever experienced it? I think we all have. This is the *disease of unbelief.* However, you say, "It's not unbelief; I believe in the Lord. I trust in the Lord. You can't say, it's unbelief." Well, if it is sin, then according to Romans 14:23 (*"Whatsoever is not of faith is sin"*) there is a sense in which it is unbelief, and it has to be dealt with.

Did you notice that this father in John chapter 4 went to the Lord and asked Him to come down and heal his son? There is a rather strange thing in John 4:48:

> *Then said Jesus unto him, "Except ye see signs and wonders, ye will not believe."*

That *not* is a double negative in Greek, which makes it

emphatic. The Lord is really saying that unless the man saw signs and wonders he would refuse to believe. Why did the Lord Jesus say that to him? I think He was testing him. Did you notice the father's reply? *"Sir, come down ere my child die."* He did not say to the Lord, "Oh, but I do have faith in you! I'm not asking for a sign." He just said that his son desperately needed help. He was not going to get into arguments. He was not asking for the sign for the sake of a sign. Here is a desperate father with a desperate cry to the Lord, and the Lord responds. He did not go to the man's home; He did something better: He spoke the word, *"Go thy way; thy son liveth."* Then it says that the man believed. Now here we have it again! When we hear the Word of God—the words of the Savior—do you know what happens? It brings faith. It engenders faith in our hearts; it helps us to believe; it just opens the door and lets a floodlight of the truth of God into our hearts. What a relief it is to have the sickness, the disease of unbelief dealt with!

The Helplessness of Unbelief

Now we go to John 5:1-3,

After this there was a feast of the Jews; and Jesus went up to Jerusalem. Now there is at Jerusalem by the sheep market, a pool, which is called in the Hebrew tongue Bethesda, having five porches. In these lay a great multitude of impotent folk, of blind, halt, withered, waiting for the moving of the water.

Verses 5-7 say,

And a certain man was there, which had an infirmity thirty and eight years. When Jesus saw him lie, and knew that he had been now a long time in that case, He saith unto him, 'Wilt thou be made whole?' The impotent man answered Him, "Sir, I have no man..."

What a cry this is: *"I have no man!"*—the *helplessness of unbelief.* Have you ever felt helpless? Indeed, the longer I go on in my Christian experience, the more helpless I feel. This is something that happens repeatedly. Well, here is a man who had been helpless for thirty-eight years. I wonder how he felt as he lay there after thirty-eight long years of illness. He had been lying at this pool day after day, and every so often, the water got all churned up. When that happened, somebody jumped in, fell in, or was thrown in, and was cured. However, the next one in, missed the blessing! Here was a man in absolute despair. So often there was the opportunity, but "I have no man." This is the *helplessness of unbelief.* The Lord, of course, healed him and we know how that happened.

That same sort of helplessness can cripple us. We are saved, yes, but let us never forget that we are only sinners, saved by God's grace. What is it that makes me helpless? Perhaps it is a question of my abilities, as I see them, against what God wants to do in me. As soon as I focus on what *I* can do and lose sight of the Lord, I become helpless in reality and will fail to allow the Holy Spirit to achieve what He could otherwise do through me. Really, it is only when we get to the place of seeing our helplessness that the Lord can take us and use us.

There were many people at the pool of Bethesda. The Scripture says there was a great multitude. They all needed healing and that is why they were there. The question begs to be asked, "Why did the Lord Jesus only heal one single man?" I suspect it might be because there was only one solitary man who recognized his helplessness and that was the beginning of new things for him. There have doubtless been times in our lives when the Lord has had to bring each of us to that place of extremity so that He can pick us up and dispel the helplessness that sometimes plagues us. As sure as we depend upon our natural abilities, we will be helpless. It is only as we rely on the Savior Himself that we will be useful to God.

We should be aware of a common trick of the devil. The thinking goes something like this: The Lord has given me a gift, and I have an obligation to use that gift. As long as I use the Spirit-given gift of God, I won't be helpless. I'll be able to do wonderful things in the service of the Lord." Well, in a sense that is true, of course. But I must not *depend on* that gift. It takes more than a gift for God's work to be done. It takes the moving of the Spirit of God, first in my heart and then, subsequently, He will be free to move in the hearts of others. This trick of the devil is to get us to look anywhere except where we should have our eyes focused. A favorite place for us to focus our attention is on our gifts. It is, in reality, unbelief, for I am not trusting in the Savior for that particular issue.

The helplessness of unbelief is like a pen. A pen is a very useful instrument. We lift the pen and write with it. We say, "That pen writes very nicely!" Have you ever seen a pen writing? A pen does not write! A pen is just an instrument that needs to be taken and guided to produce on paper the words that are in the mind of the writer. That is what we are! We are just like pens—helpless instruments, useless until the Lord lifts us up and guides us to produce the end result that He has in mind. Mind you, the pen sometimes runs out of ink, and a pen that was useful yesterday might be useless today. How we need the constant in-filling of the Spirit of God so that the Lord can lift us and use us in our condition. The Apostle Paul said it very nicely: *"...when I am weak, then am I strong"* (2 Cor. 12:10). May the Lord help us not to pretend, not to depend on other things, but only on Him. May we be increasingly available and willing to be lifted and filled with His Spirit, so that He can use us. Let us never forget this very important lesson: God can take what I think is failure and turn it to good account by His power. My helplessness, my hopelessness, my utter inability to do anything is exactly what God can use. But that is all God *can* use. Let us make sure we are in that position, that we might be useful in His service, for His Name's sake.

The Fear of Unbelief

In John 6:16-20, we find another graphic picture to take us further into this subject.

> *And when even was now come, His disciples went down unto the sea, and entered into a ship, and went over the sea toward Capernaum. And it was now dark, and Jesus was not come to them. And the sea arose by reason of a great wind that blew. So when they had rowed about five and twenty or thirty furlongs, they see Jesus walking on the sea, and drawing nigh unto the ship: and they were afraid. But He saith unto them, "It is I; be not afraid."*

It is very clear that the subject being brought to our attention in this portion is *fear.* Fear can be such a crippling thing. We have all experienced that to one degree or another in our lives.

Fear is something that characterizes the world, although there are many who would deny that! Poor people fear that they are not going to have enough to see them through the next couple of days. Rich people fear they are going to lose their wealth. Healthy people fear that they will lose their health. Ill people fear that they have come to the end of the journey. Whatever aspect of life we consider in this world, there seems to be fear on every hand. However, the Lord Jesus came to "*deliver those who through fear of death were all their lifetime subject to bondage*" (Heb. 2:15). Isn't it wonderful that death holds no fear for us? It has been conquered; the Lord Jesus has been there and come back again, so we do not need to be afraid.

Nevertheless, sometimes we are afraid. Certainly, the disciples were afraid in this story. Had we read in Matthew or

Mark's account, we would have found that the Lord Jesus had sent them away. Let us remember that the Lord has sent us. He said, *"Go ye into all the world"* and *"make disciples of all nations."* In a sense, therefore we could parallel this little portion with our own experience in life—sent away by the Lord.

Then we find that they were crossing the sea in a ship. I suppose we could say that we are crossing the sea of life. The evening has come, it is already dark, and we are looking for daybreak. We are waiting for the dawn. We sometimes sing, "I am waiting for the dawning of that bright and blessed day." Perhaps we are closer to it than we think. However, for the present it is dark. This world is a dark place, spiritually speaking. And in the darkness we find that there was a storm; a great wind blew. The difficulties of the darkness, then, are compounded by the storm, the wind, and the waves. Then we find in John 6:19 that they were rowing. Mark 6:48 tells us that they were, *"toiling in rowing."* Do we ever feel that our service for the Lord is toiling in the darkness? It will be, if we have lost the sense of His presence, as the disciples had here.

Then the Lord appeared, walking on the sea, and it says that the disciples were afraid. What were they afraid of? They were experienced seamen, fishermen—some of them at least. They had been in storms before, riding through the massive waves. This was nothing new to them. What is more, they see the Lord coming, but they are afraid! I think perhaps they did not really know who He was. Certainly, when the Lord spoke, that is the impression we get. He said, *"It is I, be not afraid."* When things are darkest and at their worst, that is always the time when the Lord makes us aware of His presence. He never permits us to go beyond that point we can bear. Sometimes we say, "I can't take any more." Well, the Lord knows whether we can take any more or not. If we can trust Him with the salvation of our souls, we can trust Him with those practical details of life. We can trust Him to know just how much we can take.

With fear often comes depression. Quite a few years ago, the Lord brought us through a very dark period of depression.

If any of you have experienced what that is like you will understand the awful feeling of uselessness, failure, and fear. It is easy to say that a Christian should never be depressed. However, if you have never been there, then might I suggest that you never, ever, tell a child of God who is in the despair and darkness of depression that he or she should not be depressed! Nothing could be better calculated to make that dear one even more depressed. Perhaps the Lord had to teach us that lesson by taking us through the experience. But, you know, *He did take us through it.* It has been perhaps one of the most valuable experiences of our lives. I say "our," because I think Dorothy suffered more than I did, trying to cope with me for those months. It has been valuable because, since that happened, the number of people that the Lord has sent into our lives who have been suffering in a similar way, with similar feelings and fears, has been remarkable. To be able to say, "I know exactly how you feel" opens people's hearts. Whatever the circumstances of life, there are several lessons that must be learned. The first is that the Lord permits and, at times, designs those circumstances to teach us lessons, to bring glory to His name, and to make us more effective in the work that He has planned for us. The Bible says: *"Perfect love casteth out fear."* John wrote that, and it is true. But sometimes we have to work our way through that sea of fear, to come out the other side, in the good hand of our God. Then we see His perfect love casting out the fear that somehow has found its way into our lives.

The Emptiness of Unbelief

A little further down in chapter 6 we read how the people were following the movements of the Lord and His disciples. When the boat got to the other side, all the people were waiting for them. John 6:25-26 reads like this:

When they had found Him on the other side of the sea, they said unto Him, "Rabbi, when camest thou hither?" Jesus answered them and said, "Verily, verily, I say unto you, Ye seek Me, not because ye saw the miracles, but because ye did eat of the loaves, and were filled."

This remark refers back to the beginning of the chapter, where we have the account of the feeding of the five thousand, and the Lord Jesus is reminding the people of what happened.

The Lord makes a very interesting statement in verse 26. He says, *"Ye seek me."* What a good thing it is to seek the Lord—in fact, the Scripture says, *"Seek ye the Lord while He may be found."* However, there is seeking the Lord, and seeking the Lord. The Lord Jesus looked into the hearts of these people and He knew they were seeking Him. But He also looked at their motives; He looked at what they desired.

Ye seek Me, not because you saw the miracles, but because you did eat of the loaves and were filled.

What is the implication of this? It is that they were empty again and had come to be filled. This is the *emptiness of unbelief.* It sums up the world in one little word: empty—utterly empty. People rush around feverishly trying to seek fulfillment, trying to fill the void of the emptiness within, and they cannot do it. Someone has said that within every human being there is a God-shaped vacuum that nothing else can fill. It is only as the Lord comes in, that such emptiness can be filled up and removed. How tragic it is when we, who have tasted of the Lord, have seen that He is good, and have known the joy and satisfaction of being filled with Christ, suddenly find that emptiness has come back. It is very real, and it happens from time to time. We sometimes sing, in that beautiful hymn, "From the best bliss that earth imparts we turn unfilled to Thee again." There is a wealth of truth in that. The best bliss that the world has to offer can never satisfy the heart that has tasted of the Savior. That is exactly what we have here in John chapter six.

The Lord Jesus said, *"I am the Bread of Life"*—the staff of life; that which not only gives life, but sustains life. See what He says in John 6:27-28,

> *Labor not for the food which perisheth, but for that food which endureth unto everlasting life, which the Son of Man shall give unto you: for Him hath God the Father sealed. Then said they unto Him, "What shall we do, that we might work the works of God?"*

It seems like they are changing the subject here, but they are not! They are following on exactly where the Lord is leading them. Why do we say that? Because, in verse 27, the Lord Jesus said,

> *Labor not for the meat that perisheth, but for the meat that endureth unto everlasting life.*

Note the word *labor.* That is the same as *work,* and then they said, *"What shall we do* [what shall we work—how shall we work], *that we might work the works of God?"* And so it follows on perfectly naturally. Look at what the Lord Jesus said in verse 29: *"This is the work of God, that ye believe on Him whom He hath sent."* We all know that we are saved by faith. We also know that we must live by faith and walk by faith. That is the message of Galatians. We start by faith, we carry on by faith, and we end by faith.

Sometimes we find that we drift back and seek to be filled with something other than the Lord. It never works! It is not that we consciously seek for these things, but we can be influenced unwittingly in this way by the world. The hymn-writer expressed it well when he said:

I tried the broken cisterns, Lord,
But ah! the waters failed;
E'en as I stooped to drink they'd fled,
And mocked me as I wailed.
Now none but Christ can satisfy,
None other Name for me;
There's love, and life, and lasting joy,
Lord Jesus, found in Thee.

Leaving Christ for anything else is unbelief and brings emptiness.

The Hatred of Unbelief

In John 7:1-2 we read:

> *After these things Jesus walked in Galilee: for He would not walk in Jewry, because the Jews sought to kill Him. Now the Jews' feast of tabernacles was at hand.*

We well know how the brothers of the Lord Jesus said to Him, "Why don't You go up to Jerusalem and show the disciples Your signs and miracles and all these wonderful things that You're supposed to be doing? Show them to the people!" And Jesus said in John 7:6-7,

> *My time is not yet come: but your time is alway ready. The world cannot hate you: but Me it hateth, because I testify of it, that the works thereof are evil.*

We now focus on the *hatred of unbelief.* Notice that the Lord Jesus spoke these words to His own brothers—that is, His own half-brothers. In fact, in verse five it says, *"Neither did His brethren believe in Him,"* and this word neither would link them with the Jews that were seeking to kill Him in verse one. What hatred this displayed!

There is nothing wrong with hatred as such. It is an emotion that God has built into our beings. Hatred cannot, of itself, be evil. I have noted down a list of some things that God hates. In Deuteronomy 16:22 we read that God hates idols and idolatry. In Psalm 45:7 we read that God hates wickedness. In Proverbs 6:16-19 we have a whole list of things that God hates: a proud look; a lying tongue; hands that shed innocent blood; a heart devising wickedness; feet that run to mischief; a false witness;

and sowing discord among brethren. In Malachi 2:16, we read that God hates divorce. Therefore, it is perfectly true that there are things we also should hate. Hatred, per se, is not wrong. We must learn to love what the Lord loves, and we must learn to hate what the Lord hates. Otherwise, we get it all topsy-turvy and the wrong way round, for the world hates what God loves and loves what God hates. We are not of the world. Indeed, we find in 1 John 2 that John warns the believers, *"Love not the world neither the things that are in the world."* Do not love it.

There is an illustration in John 18 of the importance of this. There we read of the arrest of the Lord Jesus. When they came to arrest Him, in verses 4-5, He said:

> *"Whom seek ye?" They answered Him, "Jesus of Nazareth." Jesus saith unto them, "I am He." And Judas also, which betrayed Him, stood with them.*

Please note—Judas stood with them. Here we have two groups: there is the Lord together with His disciples in one group, and the soldiers and those who have come to arrest Him in the other. Judas had to choose where to stand. Sadly, he chose to stand with them, not with the Lord.

Further down the chapter we find that the crowd has come into the High Priest's palace (v. 18):

> *And the servants and officers stood there, who had made a fire of coals; for it was cold: and they warmed themselves: and Peter stood with them.*

Isn't that sad? Oh, we can understand Judas standing with them, but Peter also stood with them! With whom? With those who hated the Savior. How tragic when we stand with the wrong people! What a terrible problem this is, because if we are with them we are going to act like them and speak like them. Shortly after this, Peter denied the Lord but he did not merely deny the Lord; he denied Him with oaths and curses. He was speaking like they were speaking. Why? Because he was standing with them. On the contrary, if we stand with the

Lord perhaps we would speak a little more like He speaks. Psalm 1:1 says:

> *Blessed is the man that walketh not in the counsel of the ungodly, nor standeth in the way of sinners, nor sitteth in the seat of the scornful.*

What a blessing! May the Lord help us to do just that.

Let us never forget that the world that hated and crucified our Savior has not changed one little bit. It still hates Him. But we love Him! If we confess that, then let us be sure we never compromise our testimony by standing along with the ungodly. This can be insidious. Surely we would never stand with them in their worldly pursuits of pleasure! Sadly, we may start to think that there are some things in the world that are somehow in a different category and we may feel happy to stand with the ungodly in these things.

One of the big issues to arise in South Africa in recent years is the question of abortion. It would be most unlikely that any of us would stand with the world in support of this legalizing of murder. However, there is a section of the community, known as the Anti-Abortion Lobby, that stands against this evil. Among such is the large Muslim community. Some dear children of God may be tempted to stand with them because the issue is right, but fail to see that the reason for the stance taken by these people is not to promote the Word of God or to honor the Lord Jesus Christ. To stand with them is to compromise and will inevitably lead to a diminishing of our effectiveness for the Lord. It is to join with them in unbelief, for they hate the Savior. This example could be multiplied many times in the various circumstances of our lives. Let us beware of the dangers and avoid repeating Peter's mistake.

The Bondage of Unbelief

In John 8:30-33 we read:

As He spake these words, many believed on Him. Then said Jesus to those Jews which believed on Him, "If ye continue in My word, then are ye My disciples indeed; and ye shall know the truth, and the truth shall make you free." They answered Him, "We be Abraham's seed, and were never in bondage to any man."

Let us stop here a moment. How ridiculous can people be! They said, *"We were never in bondage to any man!"* These were people who knew their Bibles. Had they forgotten about Egypt? What about the period of history recorded in the book of Judges? Right through the Old Testament repeatedly the people allowed themselves to be brought into bondage because of unbelief. But they had conveniently forgotten this. Our subject then is the *bondage of unbelief.* Let us go back to verses 33-34:

"We were never in bondage to any man: how sayest Thou, Ye shall be made free?" Jesus answered them, "Verily, verily, I say unto you, Whosoever committeth sin is the slave of sin."

That is the crux of the matter! They were slaves of sin. To whom was He talking? He was talking to those who believed on Him! Isn't that remarkable? It says so in verses 31-33:

Then said Jesus to those Jews who believed on Him...And they said, "We were never in bondage to any man."

Further down, in verse 44, Jesus was still talking to those same people who believed on Him, and He said, *"Ye are of your father the devil."*

That tells me that there is believing, and believing. It tells me there is a certain superficial consent to the facts regarding the person of Christ, without a deep reliance on Him for salvation. They believed, but they were of their father, the devil. Those are harsh words, but the whole point is that the Lord Jesus is showing them that they were in bondage. Let us carry on with that in verse 44:

> *Ye are of your father the devil, and the lusts of your father ye are willing to do.*

They were willing to do what their father wanted to do—in other words, what the devil wanted to do. What did he want to do? He wanted to kill the Lord and they were willing to do just that, for they hated Him. The devil

> *...was a murderer from the beginning and abode not in the truth because there was no truth in him. When he speaketh the lie* [as we saw earlier] *he speaketh of his own, for he is a liar and the father of it.*

Sin brings bondage. We have all experienced it, but this is something that we generally link with the unsaved. However, all the other features we have dealt with thus far in these studies, while linked with the unsaved, can also apply to the believer. Why should this one be different?

Is it possible for a true child of God to become a slave to sin? We do something of which we are ashamed. Then what happens? We must cover it up. Because we must be very careful not to allow it to become exposed, we become a slave to it—we are in bondage to it. It dictates how we act and how we speak. It forces us to do things that we should not have to do. If we have to hide something, the chances are it is sin and we will be in bondage to it. The big question is whether this is unbelief or not.

The Apostle Paul clearly teaches us that when Christ died He died as our Substitute. However, He also died as our Representative, and this is an entirely different but equally important truth. A representative acts not merely *for* someone else (that is a substitute), but *as* someone else. When a representative of a company signs a contract, he is legally acting *as the company.*

This was brought home to us a few years ago when we heard the story of a young man from Holland. Many years ago, he immigrated to South Africa, but his bride-to-be was unable to accompany him. Eventually, when he had secured a job and had made provision for a wife, he tried to arrange for her to join him in South Africa, only to find that the authorities insisted that she could only join him if they were married! It was, however, possible under Dutch law to arrange a marriage by proxy, and this he did. His brother represented him at the marriage, and his wife was then able to join him in South Africa. His brother was not a substitute (if he had been, *he* would have married the girl). He was the man's *representative*. He acted *as the man himself* so that, although the man was not actually at the wedding, he was deemed to be legally married because his representative acted as him.

The fact that Christ died as my Representative on the cross means that, legally in the eyes of God, I died. Paul states this in Romans 6:8-11:

> *If we died* [aorist form of the verb] *with Christ...Likewise reckon ye also yourselves to be dead indeed unto sin.*

If I permit sin to bring me into bondage, I am denying the truth of this. I am saying that I did not die, for I am still subject to sin! It is unbelief to say that, having trusted Christ as my Savior, I did not die. This will lead to sin, and bondage to this sin is the *bondage of unbelief.*

The Blindness of Unbelief

John 9:1 brings the next illustration to our attention:

And as Jesus passed by, He saw a man which was blind from his birth.

*Jesus said, 'For judgment I am come into this world, that they which see not might see; and that they which see might be made blind.' And some of the Pharisees which were with Him heard these words, and said unto Him, "Are we blind also?" Jesus said unto them, "If you were blind, you should have no sin: but now ye say, 'We see'; therefore your sin remaineth" (*Jn. 9:39-41).

What the Lord is saying here is: "If you really were blind, you could be forgiven—you would not be responsible—but actually, you say, 'We see! We understand! We know! We've got the Bible and we know God!' Therefore you are responsible!" That is the point—they were responsible. This is the *blindness of unbelief.*

Our Jewish friend, whom we mentioned earlier, constantly wonders at how blind he was when he was in Judaism. He says: "You know, I learned the Old Testament from when I was a small boy. Why could I not see what I see now?" Of course, there is a judicial blindness, because we read that God has brought a veil over the eyes of the Jewish nation (2 Cor. 3:14). We understand that refers to the nation as a whole and not to individuals. It is Satan who blinds the minds of individuals who believe not, but God has put a veil across the eyes of the Jews, nationally and judicially. Thank God, it is possible for that blindness to be removed. Just think of it! What a wonder, to be brought out of the deepest, darkest night into the glorious light of His presence! It is tremendous what God has done.

People talk about being as "blind as a bat." I do not know whether a bat is really blind or not. I only know that in experiments where bats have been blindfolded, it has not made a pin of difference to their flight. However, as soon as their ears were plugged, they were in trouble. Scientists strung a network of cords across a cave where the bats lived and the bats were able to evade all the cords and all the obstacles in their flight—until their ears were plugged. Because bats fly by sonar they could not hear the echoes and just dropped to the ground, helpless. They say that there are creatures that live in complete darkness and although they have eyes, their eyes do not function. They do not need sight in those circumstances. So it is in the world today. People are quite content to be blind. They feel they do not need anything more than they have.

Try to imagine what it would be like for you, a seeing person, suddenly to find yourself in a country where everyone was blind and not one person was able to see. Try talking to those people, not one of whom has experienced sight and has never heard of anyone who can see! You say, "Oh, isn't that beautiful?" And they say, "What are you talking about?" You say, "Just look at the sunset!" They reply: "What do you mean, *sunset?* What does *look* mean?" "Oh!", you say, "The sky is a beautiful color." The reply might well be: "Well, you are talking nonsense! What's color anyway?" They would have no concept of color, or vision, sky, sea, or mountains. That is how the ungodly are. They have no concept, not the faintest notion, of what it is like to have spiritual vision. Indeed, the idea is so foreign to them, they even deny the possibility of such a thing! It is important to remember that, when we try to bring the Word of God to these people. At times, we use phrases that are so meaningful to us and they have no idea what we are talking about! They have no spiritual vision. This is the *blindness of unbelief.*

I want to relate this to our earlier discussion on hypocrisy. This blindness was a choice these men had made. The Lord Jesus said: "Now you say, 'We see.'" This was hypocrisy. It was what they said, but it was not true. Of course, they thought they were able to see! Hypocrites can be very sincere! *We* can see the hypocrisy because they were trying to be what they were not.

Do you know what the word *hypocrite* is in Greek? The word *hypocrite* refers to an actor in Greek drama. In those days, they did not wear costumes to act out the part as actors do today. Instead, they held masks in front of their faces to represent the characters that they were acting. Indeed, in the masks there were mechanical devices to amplify their voices, otherwise they could not be heard clearly. That is what the word *hypocrite* is in Greek. It is someone who has a mask in front of them, pretending to be what he or she is not. The result is that behind the mask they are actually quite different from what they appear to be. Their claim to sight made these so-called *believers* nothing more than religious hypocrites.

In Philippians chapter two we will find one last thought connected with that point. Verses 5 and 6 say:

> *Let this mind be in you, which was also in Christ Jesus: who being in the form of God, thought it not robbery to be equal with God.*

He was in the form of God. That word *form* is the word in Greek from which we get our word *morphology,* meaning the shape of something—what it is in essence; what it is like. This word *form* is the exact opposite of the word *hypocrite.* A hypocrite is outwardly different from what he is inwardly. It is the mask in front of the actor. The word *form* in this chapter means that outwardly Christ was exactly what He was inwardly—the form of God. Then, in Philippians 2:7 we read:

> *...but* [He] *made Himself of no reputation* [He emptied Himself] *and took upon Him the form of a servant.*

This is again the same word *form.* So the Lord Jesus, in John chapter 13 when He got down on His knees to wash the disciples' feet, was not acting a part. He was a servant. He was outwardly exactly what He was inwardly. That is the force of the word. This is what God has delivered us from: that hypocrisy of wearing a mask.

Those poor Pharisees! They were sincere hypocrites! They really did think they were serving God with all their might, but they were content with the outward form. Are we? May God help us not to be, for this is the *blindness of unbelief.*

The Insecurity of Unbelief

On our journey through these first 12 chapters of John, we have now come to chapter 10. While we have done no more than refer to a few incidents in the life of the Lord Jesus, nevertheless, I trust we have had a little insight into the type of people with whom the Lord Jesus dealt. The features that marked them out are undoubtedly characteristic of modern man; and what they experienced are the same problems that inevitably beset our paths from time to time.

Many of us memorized John 10 even as children and it has remained a favorite over the years. This chapter deals with the shepherd and the sheep. Let us read verses 26-30:

> *But ye believe not, because ye are not of My sheep, as I said unto you. My sheep hear My voice, and I know them, and they follow Me: and I give unto them eternal life; and they shall never perish, neither shall any man pluck them out of My hand. My Father, which gave them Me, is greater than all; and no one is able to pluck them out of My Father's hand. I and My Father are one.*

The Lord Jesus speaks here of *My sheep.* That is a precious term. At the beginning of the chapter, the Savior was talking about the sheep. He was speaking in general terms about the fact that there are sheep, there is a sheepfold, and He is the Shepherd. However, when we come to this section, we find that He changes things a little. Here He focuses on those sheep that are His own. It is true that in verse 14 He refers to *My sheep,* but if you look carefully the word *sheep* is actually in italics—it is not in the Greek text, although understood.

However, when we come to this section the Lord is emphasizing His ownership of the sheep.

The point being made in John 10 is that there is a sheepfold. According to the custom in the villages of Palestine at that time, various people in the village, each with their little individual flock, would share one sheepfold. In the morning when they wanted to lead their sheep out, each shepherd in turn would go to the sheepfold and call his sheep, then walk away. He knew his sheep would follow him. He also knew that no other sheep would follow him. This is what the Lord Jesus is saying here: "My sheep hear My voice, and those who don't hear My voice are not My sheep!" It is so simple.

How was it that the sheep in the sheepfold recognized their shepherd's voice? Was it because each morning they heard him calling? No, that would not be sufficient—indeed, it would mean that the other sheep would then also start to recognize that voice. It was because during the day they constantly heard his voice. When a sheep gave birth to little lambs, those little lambs were brought up within the sound of the shepherd's voice, and that was the only voice they would respond to because they heard it constantly day after day. I think that is beautiful. The other sheep did not hear his voice day after day. They did not recognize it and they did not follow him. *"My sheep hear My voice, and I know them"* (Jn. 10:27). The Lord Jesus knows His sheep for the simple reason that every single day He is with them, looking at them, examining them, caring for them, speaking to them.

How do we know if someone is truly saved? It is not enough for them to have some sort of testimony. It is not enough to say, "Well, they say they love the Lord!" Anybody can say that he or she loves the Lord. I believe that there are two things that determine whether or not a person is a child of God. One of them is that they follow the Lord Jesus. The other is that God's children bear His likeness (this is dealt with later). He said, *"My sheep hear My voice...and they follow Me."* Following the Lord Jesus does not make us children of God; it merely shows that we are His sheep. That is all. That is why in verse 26 the Lord Jesus said, *"But ye believe not because ye are not of my sheep."* They were not following Him.

We see, then, that there are two types of sheep: those that are His and those that are not. That is elementary. We have seen how to determine those that are His sheep (they follow Him), but the whole point of what the Lord Jesus is saying here is that His sheep are *secure*. In essence He is saying, "My sheep are secure; I have them in My hand"—and nothing, but nothing, can take us out of His hand. By contrast, those that are not His sheep are utterly insecure. This is the *insecurity of unbelief.*

Insecurity is something else that characterizes the people in this world. They do not know where they are; they do not know where they are going—they are just lost! Insecure! People try to find security in so many different things. Someone is a good sportsman. He is competent and he knows what he is doing when he is on the sport's field. Because it gives him a sense of security, that is what he goes in for. It is possibly the only part of his life where he feels secure. Here is someone else whose eye-hand coordination is poor, so he cannot do sports—but he has a brilliant mind! He finds security in constant study and learning. He is not much good for anything else. Take him out of that environment and he is insecure. You can think of lots of other illustrations of insecurity. What is the problem? It is simply this: people in the world are looking for their security in themselves and in their own abilities. Our security is in Christ, and that is what the Lord Jesus is emphasizing here.

Sometimes even as servants of the Lord, we may feel a little bit insecure. Occasionally we become a little bewildered and wonder what is going to happen next. Why is this? It is because we have forgotten that we are sheep and that we have a Shepherd who makes us secure. Just for the moment we have lost sight of that and are like a sheep that has wandered away a little bit. It suddenly looks up to find there are no other sheep around and no shepherd in sight. That sheep will immediately start to bleat and cry to attract attention! Of course, if the shepherd is a good shepherd he will hear, and follow the sound until he finds the sheep. The Lord Jesus said, *"I am the Good Shepherd."* We only need to cry and He is there. What a wonderful Savior we have!

The Sorrow of Unbelief

Let us move to John chapter 11 and the story of Lazarus. I love this chapter for a number of reasons. One is because we read here that Jesus wept. Let us look at verse 33:

> *When Jesus therefore saw her weeping* [Mary, the sister of Lazarus], *and the Jews also weeping which came with her, He groaned in the spirit, and was troubled.*

See also verses 38-40,

> *Jesus therefore again groaning in Himself cometh to the grave. It was a cave, and a stone lay upon it. Jesus said, "Take ye away the stone." Martha, the sister of him that was dead, saith unto Him, "Lord, by this time he stinketh: for he hath been dead four days." Jesus saith unto her, "Said I not unto thee, that, if thou wouldest believe, thou shouldest see the glory of God?"*

This passage highlights for us the *sorrow of unbelief.* The capacity to sorrow is God-designed and built into us. I have had people coming to me (usually widows) who say, "I feel so guilty because of the incredible sorrow that I have." Why should they feel guilty? What is wrong with sorrowing? But there are different kinds of sorrowing, aren't there? In 1 Thessalonians 4:13 the apostle says, *"...that ye sorrow not, even as others which have no hope."* It is not that we do not sorrow! It is rather that our sorrow is of a different nature from the sorrow of the world. This is such a precious truth. The Lord does not expect us to have a stiff upper lip all the time. In fact, that could be seen as hardness. There is nothing wrong with sorrowing. However, it becomes wrong if we sorrow as those who have no hope. I think that is what was taking place in John chapter 11.

Let's go back to verse 33, where it says: *"Jesus saw her weeping, and the Jews also weeping which came with her."* It seems to me that the Lord Jesus was making a distinction here between Mary and the Jews. They were all weeping but were their tears the same? I suspect that their tears were different. Mary was weeping because her heart was broken, but the Jews were weeping because it was the thing to do. It was not necessary for either Mary or Martha to weep. But it was not wrong, and we know that because the Lord Jesus wept with them!

Why did the Lord Jesus weep? After all, He knew that in a few minutes He was going to call Lazarus out of the tomb. He was about to raise Him from the dead and He did not need to weep. Why didn't He say to Mary and Martha, "Stop weeping!"? Why didn't He say, "Look, I'm going to raise him up! I'm here to solve all your problems"? No! The Lord Jesus does not work that way, and we have all experienced that in our lives from time to time. He does not take the problems away from us. Instead He passes through the problems along with us, and that is what He was doing with these dear women. That is the sort of Savior we have. When we pass through the waters, when we walk through the fire, when the floods overwhelm us (not *if—when*) He has promised: *"I will be with thee"* (Isa. 43:2). And so the Lord Jesus said to Martha (and He said it so very gently):

> *Said I not unto thee, that, if thou wouldest believe, thou shouldest see the glory of God?* (Jn. 11:40).

He said that, not because Martha was weeping but because she was arguing! The Lord had said, *"Take ye the stone away."* We can hear Martha's doubts and concern: "But, Lord..." The Lord had to remonstrate with her very gently, but very firmly: *"Said I not...?"* How often we have to bring ourselves back to the Book and read: "Did I not say...?" We are not going to be critical of Martha because we do the same thing all the time. How good it is to know that Jesus wept with them in their grief, knowing what He was about to do—knowing the end result of it all, the glory and the rejoicing that there was going to be. The Lord Jesus shares our sorrows, our concerns, our fears and worries, knowing all that He is going to do in us and through us; knowing the end product that we cannot see. He does not say: "Don't weep!" He says: "Trust Me. Trust Me in your hour of sorrow. Trust Me in your hour of darkness. Trust Me in your despair. Trust Me in your dryness and your barrenness. Trust Me in every circumstance of your life. I am trustworthy." We have all found that repeatedly, haven't we? Why should we doubt it for one moment? Nevertheless, we do sometimes, and such unbelief brings additional sorrow that we could well do without!

The Selfishness of Unbelief

Let us move over to John chapter 12, the last chapter we are going to look at. There are some very sad things in this chapter. At the beginning, we have one of the most beautiful little sketches in the whole gospel of John. It is the incident where Mary takes the ointment and pours it over the feet of the Lord Jesus in a delightful act of worship. However, that is not what I want us to consider. Let us read verse 6, that dark verse which almost spoils the whole picture.

> *This he* [Judas] *said, not that he cared for the poor; but because he was a thief and had the bag, and bare what was put therein.*

We remember Judas had said, *"Why was not this ointment sold for 300 denarii and given to the poor?"* Why should she waste it like that? We have heard that sort of thing in our own lives, haven't we? Why do you have to go away to some remote corner of the earth and waste your life? Waste it? The Lord Jesus said, "If you save it, you've lost it! If you give it, you've gained it!" There is nothing wasted that is given to the Lord Jesus. Nothing! We can give our money to Him; it is not wasted. We can give our intelligence to Him; it is not lost. We can give our strength, our time, whatever—it is never wasted.

Why did Judas think it was wasted? Because he thought he should have it! It is not what he said that was wrong, but what he thought. He said: "We could sell it and give it to the poor." But what he was thinking was: "We could sell it and give it to me!" That is what the Word says; we are not reading anything into it. He was a thief; he had the bag and he kept all that was in it. That is why he said what he did. This is the *selfishness of unbelief.*

This is something else that marks out the worldling. We live in a very selfish world. Almost everyone in the world is looking out for "number one." The way to get on in the world is to trample others into the mud and climb on top of them.

Let's never forget that we have a Savior who was utterly selfless. What a pattern He has left for us! We only need to pay another visit to the cross, and there we can see irrefutable evidence of the absolute selflessness of the Lord Jesus Christ. Picture the scene as they throw the lovely Savior to the ground and nail His hands and feet to the wooden structure. Hear His words, *"Father, forgive them."* Wasn't that selflessness? He was not thinking of the pain He was suffering. He was thinking of those cruel soldiers who were hammering the nails through His hands. He was thinking of how they would be lost forever if they did not trust Him. So He prayed, *"Father, forgive them."* He was utterly selfless.

I can imagine what happened when the two thieves were thrown to the ground and nailed to their crosses. I can see the struggling, the wrestling, the shouting, crying, and screaming as they cursed those who were treating them so vilely. But not our Savior! I see Him lifted up there on that cross, struggling to breathe. Think of the excruciating pain as He hung suspended there. Then He looks down, and sees His mother. He loves her dearly and talks to her and to the disciple John: *"Woman, behold thy son...son, behold thy mother."* Every extra breath He had to take meant added agony, but He was utterly selfless and did His duty in caring for His mother. Maybe we could understand that, but can we understand His concern for the thief beside Him? *"Today shalt thou be with Me in paradise."* In His utterly selfless way He had compassion on a self-confessed criminal and had time to speak words of comfort to him. This was in stark contrast with Judas, who only thought about himself.

In 2 Timothy 3:2 we find a list of nineteen descriptive terms relating to people in the end times. The item that heads the list is: *"lovers of their own selves."* That means they will be selfish; just the situation in the world today. The tragedy is when it becomes true in our lives as those who love the Lord. Again, we remind our hearts of how important it is to *"follow His steps"* as Peter puts it in 1 Peter 2:21.

The Hardness of Unbelief

In John 12:37-41, we read:

> *But though He had done so many miracles before them, yet they believed not on Him: that the saying of Isaiah the prophet might be fulfilled, which he spake, "Lord, who hath believed our report? And to whom hath the arm of the Lord been revealed?" Therefore they could not believe* [please notice that—they *could not* believe], *because that Isaiah said again, "He hath blinded their eyes, and hardened their heart; that they should not see with their eyes, nor understand with their heart, and be converted, and I should heal them." These things said Isaiah, when he saw His glory and spake of Him.*

Isn't that a wonderful Scripture? Isaiah, hundreds of years before the birth of the Savior, saw His glory and spoke of Him.

This is the *hardness of unbelief.* Now, we have a problem here that we must consider. You will notice that these people had their hearts hardened by God so that they *could not* believe. That presents a problem to some, but it is there and we must deal with it. This scripture must be balanced with 1 Timothy 2:4 where it is specifically stated that God desires that all should be saved.

In the Old Testament story of Israel as slaves in Egypt, we read on a number of occasions that Pharaoh hardened his heart. We also read that the Lord hardened Pharaoh's heart. If you examine very carefully that portion of scripture in Exodus 7:1–14:8, you will find that the Lord spoke to Pharaoh repeatedly. Each time God spoke to Pharaoh, the king hardened his heart.[1] This happened no less than six times. Finally, the Lord as much as said: "All right! If that's the way you want it, that's the way it's going to be!" At that point, the Lord hardened

Pharaoh's heart. From then on in the narrative, on six occasions it is recorded that the Lord hardened Pharaoh's heart. There came a time in the life of Pharaoh when God had decided that he would have no further opportunity to change his mind. He had chosen and God now confirmed his choice eternally by hardening his heart.

That is what we have in John chapter 12. These men had heard the Lord Jesus; they had seen the signs He performed; they had opportunity to trust Him, to believe on Him. What an incredible privilege was theirs! Yet, they hardened their hearts. At this stage, the Lord Jesus had come to the end of His public ministry. He would no longer speak to anyone, apart from His own disciples. What was happening here was that these people had hardened their own hearts and the Lord was confirming their choice: they could not believe. People are on record as having prayed for individuals for fifty years and more. We often wonder how it is that someone, prayed for so faithfully, can be lost. Doubtless, the Lord speaks to such, but there comes a time—and we do not know when it is—when the Lord confirms a person's choice to them and they cannot turn back. They have passed the point of no return. That point of time is for the Lord to decide. Therefore, we continue to pray for, and preach the gospel to, the unsaved. That is our responsibility. How solemn is the *hardness of unbelief.*

Sadly, it is possible that what characterized those people can characterize us. Hardness can also come into our hearts. And when we find such hardness, it should speak to us because it can only come from one source. Let us go back again to chapter 8:44:

> *Ye are of your father the devil, and the lusts of your father ye* [are willing to] *do.*

Remember that these were religious people. Why did the Lord Jesus say, *"Ye are of your father the devil"*? Because what characterized them was what characterized the devil—in this case, hatred. Sometimes in our lives, we can find that which does not characterize the Lord. We only have two choices: we can be a child of the devil or a child of God. We are children of God by faith in the Lord Jesus Christ. How do we know? We have already seen that following Him proves we are His sheep. Now we are dealing with the second point, and I believe it is a vital one.

We find the information in Romans 8:12-16:

> *Therefore, brethren, we are debtors, not to the flesh, to live after the flesh. For if ye live after the flesh, ye shall die: but if ye through the Spirit do mortify the deeds of the body, ye shall live. For as many as are led by the Spirit of God, they are the sons of God. For ye have not received the Spirit of bondage again to fear; but ye have received the Spirit of* [sonship], *whereby we cry, "Abba, Father." The Spirit Himself beareth witness with our spirit, that we are the children of God.*

A very important thing about children is that they bear certain characteristics of the parent. By the way, when we study our New Testament we should note where it says *children,* and where it says *sons,* because the two words mean different things![2] Unfortunately, the KJV does not translate the words consistently. Children (*sons* in the Bible terminology) reproduce family characteristics and this is the second great proof that a person is truly a child of God: the character of God is, in some little way, reproduced in that person.

Of course, we still have that old nature and sometimes the old character can come to the fore. It is our choice: are we going to reflect that old side of our character (the darkness, barrenness, joylessness, hypocrisy, dullness, dryness, disease, helplessness, emptiness, hatred, bondage, blindness, insecurity, sorrow, selfishness, hardness of unbelief)? Are these the things that will be displayed in our lives? Or are we going to reflect what the Lord Jesus has done for us in saving us from all these things? We have a wonderful Savior who is absolutely sufficient for every circumstance of life. We do not know what lies ahead. We do not know what sorrow there might be. We do not know what darkness and despair may cross our paths. We do not know what sense of helplessness and emptiness we may have to face. However, we are assured of this mighty fact, that whatever comes our way, our Savior is sufficient. He is utterly trustworthy. May God help us to keep that in the forefront of our minds for His glory.

ENDNOTES

1 The first reference in Exodus 7:13—as it appears in the KJV—seems to indicate that the Lord hardened Pharaoh's heart. However, the Hebrew text does not, apparently, support this and a better translation is "Pharaoh's heart was hardened." This is the meaning conveyed by most, if not all, of the major translations including: RV; JND; NASB; NIV; AMP. BIBLE; MOFFATT, etc.

2 An example that illustrates the distinction between the two is found in Ephesians 2:1-3. In verse 2, the term *children of disobedience* should be *sons of disobedience,* while in verse 3 *children of wrath* is correct. *Sons of disobedience* signifies that those in question were characterized by disobedience. *Children of wrath,* on the other hand, signifies those who were destined to experience the wrath of God. Compare this with Mark 3:17 where James and John were called the *sons of thunder*—it was what characterized them. In Romans 9:8, we have reference to *children of the promise,* and here it is destiny that is in view.

Scripture Index